NOTES ON LEAVING

NOTES ON LEAVING

∽

L A I S H A   R O S N A U

NIGHTWOOD EDITIONS

ROBERTS CREEK, BC

2004

Nightwood Editions
R.R. #22, 3692 Beach Ave.
Roberts Creek, BC
Canada VON 2W2

Edited for the house by Silas White
Typesetting by Carleton Wilson

We gratefully acknowledge the support of the Canada Council for the Arts and the British Columbia Arts Council for our publishing program.

NATIONAL LIBRARY OF CANADA CATALOGUING IN PUBLICATION

Rosnau, Laisha, 1972–
        Notes on leaving / Laisha Rosnau.

Poems.
ISBN 0-88971-200-X

        I. Title.

PS8585.08336N68 2004   C811'.6   C2004-901180-4

CONTENTS

PART I:

POINT OF EXIT

ॐ

Already

1.

My cousins from the prairies believe
that we live on top of a mountain,
say roads unroll like ribbons
into valleys on either side.

Perched on this peak, we balance
bike seats, tips of sneakers become
pliant kickstands on pavement,
sweat slicks handgrips under palms.

I instruct, there will be no brakes
until the bottom. *All ready?*
Wind as clean and sharp as pins
in pores, red streamers flame

from the handlebars. I backpedal,
wait for the squeal of tires,
but motion freewheels in the spokes
and my brakes do not catch.

Fearing movement without end,
I steer myself into a fence post,
weighted to the ground with dirt,
end my flight, meet it with my face.

2.

We sleep, six kids to the camper,
door open for the heat and the restless
dog we are sure will protect us.
It is the sound we hear first –

the dull roar of a mountain on fire
as the dog barks at the rumbling
bank of orange and the horse
goes crazy for the smoke.

Adults stumble onto the lawn
in bathrobed awe, steer crying
cousins back into the house,
coddle them with fold-out couches.

My brother and I choose the camper.
Bravery-bound, wise, we know
that the mountain is always
farther away than people think;

that we live on top of a hill,
a valley between us and the burning,
the fence posts holding
everything in place.

In the morning, there is blood
on the pillow where I rested
my cheek, scraped and marked
with yesterday's accident.

The fire is out. A black patch flowers
on the mountain and the smell of smoke
is old in the air. My skin stings
but it has begun to scab already.

WONDERLAND

She pretends to read in the back of the car,
Disney books, thin and coded with colour –
the white of milk-sweet girls, true love
in a bead of crimson blood. She stares down
pictures until they blur: fairies become smudged
bugs on the windshield, a prince morphs
into a twisted plastic bag, tumbles
along the side of the highway. She listens
to taped voices, turns pages when she hears
the sound of a tinkling waterfall (hand
clamped between her legs when
she has to pee).

These books are not full of the words
she finally learns to read. Instead,
somewhere on the prairies, she looks
out the window and understands the sign.
Understands that the backwards 3 is an E,
that, with the curl of two snakes
and a circle moon, this spells ESSO.
She holds the knowledge in her mouth,
releases the shapes of words to the reflection
of her lips in the car window.

She will tell you this story later,
the back seat thick with baggage, the dog
stinking in the heat. She will tell you one
too many times as your road trips blur together,
the lights on the signs in each new small town
no longer winking like bright promises.
When you pull over at gas station restrooms,
you will light a cigarette while she goes, spell
her name on air with the cherry, stamp
it under foot when she gets back into the car.

Lucas

Your tactics from the first house: kicks
to the shin, biting whatever skin or bone
you could between teeth as small as pearls.
Mine: pulling hair – held tight, tiny points
of scalp near release – running, screaming.

In the second house, the torment
we rained on each other led us
to sit side by side on the couch,
struck dumb and stiff as balled fists,
as we watched Mom cry. Knowing it was us.

The third: battles with things that shone.
Kitchen blades held in clean lines
under fluorescent light until one of us or the other
broke and bolted – backdoor, barefoot, driveway –
neither going far. Knocking knives from hand

to the ground all that mattered. Under tire and boot,
utensils dulled over seasons of being left to the gravel.
In that same house, a gleaming silver tea service sent
flying, my grip released with your head in mind.
Arc of cream, fine spray of sugar dust fell

as the silver missed my intended target.
And those fake crystal knobs on the doors –
I kicked you when you were already crouched,
your head a resonant crack against the prism,
hate refracting from your eyes.

One more move and I was out, this time
not a house, but an apartment in the city – full
of boys, foam mattresses moulding to the floors,
a grocery cart of empties in the closet –
where I sent you letters from the world.

Holy shit, you should see the fireworks here.

The 'hydro' in the bill actually refers to electricity.

When you leave, try to go farther than this city. It can stop you.

We are each running out of ways to count
the houses lived in since. We meet where moving
people do – airports, bus stops, other peoples'
places – and then get into cars, dare
each other to speed. Consistent, smooth runs.

We'll compare scars, none inflicted
by one another, and watch for potential roadkill.
We'll slow down when the sun goes, our faces
reflected off dark glass, the way our eyes
point up, grins crack, the same.

How Babies Are Made

You read the book with your mother,
take turns, push the words
over your lips, then watch
as they pass through hers,
surprised that you can both make
the same sounds by moving
your eyes over the page.

By yourself, you curl into the mattress
under the basement stairs, read:

> *The man and woman lie very close together*
> *in the bed and hug. The man puts his penis*
> *inside the woman's vagina.*

You climb the stairs, cramp words
like question marks inside you, ask
    Do grown-ups really do this?
and
    How does that feel?
Your mother's response furls, unfurls
in your mind –
    Very good. If you're married.

Your friend's cat gives birth in a box
under the table on the patio.
You tell Cindy about the way
babies are made, the words big
between you   *Penis*
Regina   until you both wonder
who Muffin married.

You and Cindy are too small
to close the latch on the patio gate.
You watch and scream while King,
the German Shepherd, eats
the baby kittens, the sound
of small bones between his teeth
louder than any word you've read.

Haircut, Age Eleven

Trapped between skin and rib,
they appeared overnight,
hard and sore

and she had no way of knowing
what they might be, even though she
had listened all through Sex Ed,

had learned about blood
and hormones – no one
had said anything

about stones on the chest
and what else could she assume
but breast cancer?

When she was sure the cancer
was growing, her chest swelling
with infection, she told her mother

who tried to soothe her with the truth,
and she wanted more than ever
to carve those tumours out

– impossible, so she followed her brother
to the barbershop in the mall
had her hair cut until it was

short and close to the head,
until she could feel her skull
round and certain

when she raised her hands,
not wanting to touch herself
anywhere else.

The Girls Are Sleeping

The girls are sleeping, books splayed out
around them. Lips parted,
they take in air in quick small sips

like soda up a straw. I like to believe
they are innocent but I know how I am
around them, lips parted,

words held, hot frustration. Myself, age eleven:
tart candy stuffed on quick fingers into hip pockets.
They *are* innocent but I know how I was then

with bright girl lips and wide eyes, the knowledge that
I could attract anyone I wanted, slip them in
like tart candy stuffed on quick fingers into hip pockets.

My girls are sharp readers; I know
they find the good parts, laugh themselves asleep.
I can still attract anyone I want, slip them in

late, tuck them into my bed while I check to see if
the girls are sleeping, books splayed out.
They found the good parts, laughed themselves asleep,
taking in air in quick small sips.

And Sweeter Still

The wind through apple trees
seeps screens into bedroom windows.
I wake to breeze bruised with fruit,

am drawn downstairs to the kitchen, hum
of the fridge, light hollowed out, grey.
I cross still-warm linoleum,

open the door to let air wander the house,
hear small sounds under the deck, jump
with the bang of the screen,

stamp my footprints into dewed grass,
go down on knees and hands
looking for suddenly silent frogs.

I want only to hold one, wet
against my cheek, want to sleep there,
light striping me later with morning.

Public Swim

Summers, we don't swim in public
pools where I come from.
There are lakes, we brag,
everywhere. Three are spitting
distance from town, and several
people have backyard pools.

In northern Alberta, things
are different. It isn't as flat
as you might expect. Hills roll,
for example, and rivers duck
low in valleys. It is surprisingly
warm in the summer. However,

there are storm clouds of mosquitoes
in the sky. Biblical things happen.
I swear, every seven years while lying
on your back in a public pool, you can close
your eyes and hear, clear through the water,
swarms of locusts in fields and trees.

Pay attention to your surroundings.
If you don't, a boy might swim
under you, pull at your suit, and poke
his fingers around under there, between
your legs. That is something
that you might not expect either.

ON THE GROUND

You are on a foam mat
in your best friend's basement, counting
to one hundred, slowly, wishing
you could skim part of yourself off.

You already know that certain women
can divide. Grade 11 Psychology
has taught you that some can split
from within, tear a twin out,

whole and invisible as an atom,
while the body waits, heavy
and tractable in hands that smell
of dirt, chalk, vinegar. Hands that press

silence like inky fingerprints into skin
until those girls and women split again – quavers
and semi-quavers rising up around their bodies,
humming to distract. You know all this

by the time he spreads your legs, puts his mouth
there. You wish you could hover near
the low ceiling, see the open legs and buried head
as just that – two limbs and a skull

– but you watch the television glow
on his shoulder, a sleek hump,
not from up there but from where
you are, on the ground.

POINT OF EXIT

Let us return then, to the bathroom
of Tim Hortons, the first equation
of inebriation – one two-sixer, three
girls, straight down. Let us return
to everything that followed, a night
like mercury – metallic taste
in mouths, figures nimbus-lined,
time a slow, smooth drop.

Let us return to where we lined up to enter
a community dance, too young then to understand
nausea, the room spun out, a wheel of sparks
off us, and all we could think was
Let it always be like this. Later, watch
as we drape over chairs, necks stretched
taut between weight of hair, heft
of hearts, as we each hold the smooth
beating fish of boys' tongues
in our mouths and we think, *It will be.*
It will be like this.

When you return with us there,
you will hear it – in the squeak
of our tight throats between words,
in the whistle of air we take into
our nostrils, pink-rimmed and dry,
in the knock of bones
when our knees have forgotten
which way is forward – you will hear:
We have to go now. Let's get out of this place.

PART II:

A ROCK BALLAD

∽

What Dads Do

Dads leave suburbs by train,
go to the city, come back scented
with other, non-home, things: elevators,
cigarettes, Scotch. Sometimes they bring
home TVs sold office-to-office by guys
from the Italian Quarter named Gio.
And we all know, it isn't in the offices
that the real dads are. Instead,
they are back there, ducking
out of duty, selling cats to Chinese
restaurants for extra cash, learning how to shift
Chevies on the Back 40 so they can
get the hell out of Dodge.

Dads are sneaking out at night
down trails into the bush to where they hide
smokes and girlie mags. One night,
one dad, yours, shocks an owl on the path
and it rears up, beats him with wings as strong
as a grown man's open fists, reminds your dad
that sometimes the things that look so pretty
and still perched up high by day
can be dangerous at night.

Charlie

I was busting out

of Jordaches with new hips, hardly anything really, but more than the bones tense with skin that had been there before. Under the appliqué of my tight t-shirt (*tigerlily* in silver letters) my nipples were hard rocks, always aching, and my mind farther away than field and farm and the boys that hid in the barn with curses and dirty words, promising cigarettes for favours. I could find my own smokes, thank you very much, on top of the same dresser from where I cleared change, slid it into tight pockets, the edges of coins showing clean through denim, could strike a pose with your heels taken from the closet, his cigarette perched in my mouth, in front of the master bedroom mirror before slipping things out.

But I never went far,

it seems, just leaned against the west side of the house where there was no sun, no yard, crouched over dirt, shielded by the wood pile, three cords high, lit up, and flipped open my pick of the day – *Playboy, Penthouse, Hustler* – my favourites honey-haired, round-hipped girls from the Seventies, daisy-chained and spread, banded with sunlight through the raised roofs of haylofts. The taste of smoke in my mouth, their thighs, my light head got me high and I sprayed the air with your Charlie perfume when I was done to lift me higher.

You must've known.

I probably stank of both smoke and perfume – but then, you may have understood that I was keeping myself from the boys in the barn, that those boys could never give me moments so light. You must have hoped that I would leave that place unscathed, never falling for taunts and lures, invitations into backseats and truck-beds. That I would follow a trail of Charlie perfume and magazine promises out of town. You were right, of course, about so many things, but I could sure use a cigarette now. Don't worry, I've quit, and besides, I would never smoke in front of you.

CAVE

Sliding, slim-limbed,
into the crevice in the rock,
I imagine I am sandpaper,
the stone as supple as skin.

When I scrape myself,
it is my own roughness rising
to the surface, the part of me
that grates at things: my mother's nerves,
my brother's arm tracked with my nails.

Through this passage I come
to a ledge where the rock is stained
black, a permanent shadow,
the size of a body curled
to hide from heat.

Vertigo releases the brink underfoot
and I slide back into the gap
that will return me to the path.
Halfway through, a garter snake
blunts her head on the air

in front of my face, tongue flicking
out, in. I stare her down, slip out,
sidestep the rock pile where snakes coil,
walk the field home to have wounds
dabbed with witch-hazel.

Every eleven-year-old has a twin.
Mine braids grass through the fields,
at night returns to lie on stones, the tongues
of garters on her skin as she hollows herself
into a cave, becomes the dark.

Night Swimming

When the lake pulled us
from the dock,
swift-bodied and drunk,
we already knew

how it would feel
when weeds wound slick
around our ankles, pulled
us farther into water
which had no measurable depth
only layers of darkness,

knew how it would feel
when, one by one, we would
jerk our ankles free, split
the lake's surface
mouths gaping.

What we didn't know was this:

    Christine would sell sex in Germany;
    Jen would waitress until the day
    her tongue twisted over the specials,
    struck dumb with monotony;
    Tanya would love women
    and be hated for it;

    that we would each forget
    how the air would dry the flat, smooth
    skin first, how we could harbour
    lake water for hours in our hair, beneath
    our breasts, between each toe.

We crawled back to the dock,
cuffs of imagined green
staining our ankles and we knew
how it felt to lie open to the night,
nothing holding us under.

STASH

Tickle in the gut, warm feeling
of stars between legs, centre
folded out between us, little
brother and sister, bare naked
ladies our secret, found between
pages piled in a forgotten shed.

I invited someone else in –
the toughest, sassiest girl
in grade three – longed to impress
with glossy pages, sports car
and hi-fi stereo ads, the pact
of breasts, of teeth and hair
so straight and strong I thought:
horses.

She stared, open-mouthed
then stood, hands between legs,
cried *I feel funny*, and that was the end
of that. No brother, no schoolgirl
partner in porn, I was on my own
to follow the looped handwriting
of sweet centrefolds, wonder
what I would list as hobbies.

ONE OF HER CHILDHOODS

She pulls away when I grab her
by the wrist, my fingers
a half-moon hold around bone;
her sudden movement, a bird

startled from its nest. She cradles
hand to chest like an injury,
as though if she didn't
it would fly, slap my face.

Don't. A man used to take her
like that, she tells me. I won't
understand until later.

She curls fingers around a fine wand,
dips it in wax, forms buds, stamens,
criss-crosses along shells. Soaked in dye,
the eggs will tell me stories of her

other childhood, the one she wants
to remember, and I will memorize
the patterns, trace ridges
across eggshells, always careful.

Hestia

You were prescribed as a cure,
a pregnancy a prairie doctor hoped
would reform your mother's condition,

and came into a place where the work
was continuous, your mother did not die
and you became the medicine.

It wasn't the dates your older sisters
went on that you envied,
but their role as sons.

Your sisters were able to kill
animals, to skin and dismember,
know the heat of muscle and vein.

They were able to play pranks
with internal organs, to run in mock horror
across the yard, spotted with blood.

You had to remain a daughter, the youngest,
eggs collected in your arms, the smell
of milk souring always about you.

When your sisters left, taken
by marriage, your father hired hands,
you helped Mother in the kitchen.

It would be years before the first
half-ton truck drove by your farm
but you knew then what you wanted:

the control of something so large;
to hold the gears in your hand
and shift.

REQUEST

As I danced, a man said,
I want to see you naked.
He couldn't know that after years
of letting him in, I might turn away,
pull the sheet off the bed,
wince as though my skin ached
when exposed to words.

I catalogue each in a notebook:
name, age, occupation, what got me
into beds and out again.
Sometimes, when I watch you
across a table, I see it all: reluctance
snapping like fabric until it rips
into the willingness to undress,
willingness to leave. A list
with your name almost on it.

I want to see you naked,
as though we are still allowed
to say things like this. No thought
to exile from the garden
or wars waged within the lexicons
of sex. Who could know
that I would admire him for that?
That it would become a hand
along the backbone of this poem?

Despite those words, this fumbling
discourse like drug-laced fingers
struggling with the clasp of a bra,
he never did see me naked –
and you might not either. But,
let me tell you this: we live in a world
saturated with symbolism. Sometimes,
it is best to be direct.

PROPHET RIVER

You are teaching me to drive. No surprise,
I believe I know it all. This van, a rattling relic
of another era. Me, a danger behind the wheel.

The highway begs acceleration, denies reproach,
so swallow speed with the hiss of tires, Catherine-wheels
of spray, suck it up with the sudden drops, sharp hits

of sensation in your groin. A woman crests
the ditch, thumb raised, and I take a long time
to slow down, back up. You slide open the door.

When I practice my pass – swerve to the wrong side
of the road, jerk back again – she screams, pinballs
off worn upholstery, scraps of carpet, uncovered metal.

The woman wants out at the side of the highway
but we doubt her ability to walk and drive her home –
a bushed crescent lined with identical shacks.

Children circle the van, press inward – split lips,
cauliflower ears, crossed eyes. The alcohol
they've not yet drank already marks them.

I open my door and they climb onto my lap,
take turns pounding the horn before we leave
the woman, all of them, there. They are home,

after all. When I start to cry, the centre line
blurs and I take on the road like a quarrel
while you complain of hunger.

Fort Nelson is a strip of highway adorned
with gas pumps and diner food. We'll stop there
so that you can eat. Then we will keep going.

Girls on the Farm: A Rock Ballad

Three years after leaving you, she is back, just
passing through. The smell of sunblock lifts off her
skin, meets the mildewed walls of your rented farmhouse.
Her backpack a lump at the end of the bed.

Once, you thought the scope of your desire could cast
her as a callow rock-and-roll wife, learning
to cook hot curries in the kitchen while your band
forced riffs into the guestroom-cum-studio.

Now, you notice how when she touches
those foam walls she doesn't respond
to the notes lodged there, how in the yard her eyes
keep drifting to that place in the barn;

the place where your landlord's daughter,
a sinuous twist of a girl, hung herself
three years ago, perhaps while you thought
of the girl here now and beat off, palm raw with it.

Soon, she too will be a memory, bending
to accommodate her bags as she leaves you
again for the next bus south. After she is gone,
you will write a song, one inspired not by her

but by the girl in the barn, how she taught you
that girls leave and when they do their absence
becomes a place that hands on neither cock
nor guitar can reach.

SPAWNING

When you don't call that weekend
I feed to the stray cat at my door
a jar of canned salmon,

one of your last gifts – caught,
cleaned, smoked, and sealed
into glass jars while I wrote,

my fingers agile on the keyboard
no longer accustomed to dirt, bark,
the sting of blade when I would cut myself

while opening wood or skinning scales.
We traced our patterns over the map
– our lives together a triangle,

the points: coast, interior, north.
We used each other's absences
as a compass, as direction itself.

The salmon sat on my bottom shelf,
uneaten while I wrote one last paper
and you refolded the map.

The small planes you fly must land here
at some point but you leave before the city
lights remind you that I am still on the ground.

I go down to the water and think
of salmon that once spawned
so thick the rivers were red with them.

How bloody and ragged they were
when they reached their river;
how they knew when they were home.

PART III:
BEG AND CHOOSE

෭

(UNHIDDEN)

see how the girl crouches
on the ventilation grate, blue
plaid twisted, stuck
to pubescent thighs (thin
as fine birch.)

her face masked, spine,
a foetal curve. she licks
salt tears from her knees,
knowing she isn't hidden –
a caged spectacle of fear.

she blurs between
her wet, gathered lashes
the faces of other
children who watch
but sees one girl's pink

knuckles tight on the bar
that separates grate
from playground, hears
her speak quietly, words falling
between slats of rising steam.

CENTRAL STANDARD

We take turns showering, then neither of us
dry off, moisture our defence. We drip
prints around your apartment, thin slips
stick to us, first with water,
then with sweat.

I am not used to the heat, the time zone,
and you tell me to sleep in your bedroom
during afternoons, the fan filtering sounds
of kids calling from the schoolyard,
a slim street away.

The walls are tracked with wine-coloured
trails where you rolled paint, the sponge
prints still visible, giving everything
texture, closing like velvet
around me with the heat.

Your sheets are twisted, the night
sweat dry, the pattern of your lover
and you together erased with the code
of my own body, tossing. I sleep now
so that we can be awake together later.

When I get up, we go to the fire escape,
drink beer from wineglasses, tease the cat
with cigarettes. We each snag our vintage
bawdy house slips on rough parts
of the wrought-iron bars.

When your boyfriend comes home,
we call to him, show him our ripped
satin, tell him that when he goes out
for more beer, to bring back matches,
please. We aren't going anywhere,

and the night? It is young and we will
hold it right here, between us.

CELEBRATION

Her lover was a bicycle mechanic
in a shop on the quay. Once a fish
market, there was a salmon
painted on the outside, twisted
in mid-leap, gills gleaming.

When she left him, we joined her
one night, tried to spray-paint
a bicycle under the fish,
the challenge of such a large
project and difficult subject

discouraging. Though we were
there for support, we fought
over paint cans like girls,
then agreed she should be the one
to put the writing on the wall:

A woman needs et cetera.

Later, we mounted the first Skytrain
of the morning, belligerent
with caffeine and solidarity, though
none of us felt as clever as we had wanted,
and none of us admitted this.

We had read somewhere that the bicycle
helped to liberate women. Ankles revealed,
bloomers flashed in the ability to move
solely by one's will and strength, bike seats
hard and certain between legs.

We decided that, if this was true,
then driving a stick shift
must be all the more so, and a couple
of us offered to lend her our cars,
help move her stuff out of his place.

She insisted she didn't want to. Told us
that she had a new job and could replace
everything, piece by piece. We went out
for dinner to celebrate, raised glasses, laughed
until our bellies were sore with it.

Milking

Three times a week she wakes him
early to milk the goats, shakes his shoulder,
her hands rough with wood split, twigs
twisted into baskets, pads of her fingers
smooth with the daily turn and pull
of braided hide through beads.

He is thicker now with each winter –
the weight of traplines, dog teams, the echoes
of shots through trees gaining on him,
rings on a split tree – but he gladly
enters milking mornings,
closes the door between the cabin
rounded with stoved warmth

and sharp white silence. Steps to the barn
mark darkness with squeals of snow.
Goats' pupils shrink under propane lamps,
straight lines clean as the slice of sun
along the horizon, denied the full bowl
of light by the tilt of the earth.

He cups his hands around them, stretched warm
with milk. The move together, slow method
of their jaws, his hands pumping in rhythm,
and it is then that he tells the goats things:
How, in less than a month, the sun will bounce
from one mountain to another in only two hours.

How he's been drinking too much again. How
on mornings when he doesn't milk he lies
in bed and wishes he were small enough that she,
the mistress of these goats, could roll him
like a bead, smooth and round and whole
between the pads of her fingers.

WHAT I WANT:

Someone who calls me
by my last name, wrestles
as a form of affection, holds
my arm behind my back,
asks, *Do you give up now?* nicely.

Someone who tells jokes
that are slightly unacceptable,
never waters things down,
takes no offence to sarcasm, and
occasionally makes fun of children.

Someone who doesn't doubt
that my success may not come easily
but that it will come quickly, a swift
blow padded with cash; who will
encourage me to spend frivolously.

Someone who says *You stay right
there, I'll do it*, but never doubts
my ability to swing an axe, gut
a fish, mow a lawn, lift heavy things.
Who respects outward inactivity.

Someone who believes
that insomnia is a suture, the night
a way to bring the coarse
edges and the smooth together,
knows the unrest this can cause.

Someone who unapologetically
takes to my body like a drug –
like something that creates its own
hunger, demands supplication,
and makes a bed of foolhardy decisions.

Someone who will never be sorry;
for whom this addiction, insomnia,
indolence, frivolity, sarcasm,
and twisted arms will become a place
to rest, hold steady, then yield.

KEEPING TIME

The last two lines are taken from Richard Wilbur's "Love
Calls Us to the Things of the World"

I bottled my own blood,
one red week masoned in the fridge,
while you shrugged off ritual, feared
mistaking it for beet juice,
and kept packing.

Later, you call from a wet
corner of Asia, monsoon-soaked
on a river between Vietnam
and Cambodia, and tell me
you've been shot at from shore,

fishermen casting bullets
over water like line
with weapons from a war
you and they both
know you didn't fight.

You tell me how the nuns chose
that moment of fire to slip
their boat between yours
and the bank, crimson
robes a gliding armour.

They told you to follow, led you
up a jungle path. In the distance,
they blurred, spots of red, bright
poppies, and you spent more days
than you wanted with them,
prone with fever.

When I pick you up at the airport,
you are still too sick to realize
that the loose cotton clothes covering
your thin skin won't warm you here.
How could you forget our weather?
I won't tell you,

not yet, that I've stopped
bleeding. That the months
you've been gone I've been
counting the days like a rosary,
bottling something within me.

While you were away,
I didn't wash the sheets.
Three months and the smell
of you faded just days before
your return. We gather

it all on the bed – sheets, cotton clothing,
t-shirts stained yellow with sweat –
scatter spores of dust, and I pray:
For you and me, for now
Let there be nothing on earth
but laundry.

LEGACY

Anger is an acquired trait.
There are those who split it up
like sourdough starter or flint,
a piece of something that can grow,
rise, suck up air.

And those who pass it on, pawn
tickets to ride the mainline
past desire, share needles
and, for warmth, heavy blankets
speckled with disease.

And then there are those we fear
we are, who play our anger like a game –
a medicine ball heaved – grateful
the weight has left our hands, calculating
how to pass it off, avoid being hit.

BEG AND CHOOSE

Held up to pale light,
the burst condom dripped,
smeared your thighs. I etched
letters into the salt milk,
formed one word.

I roll clothing into balls until
my pack is full, count backwards
to the last clots and wonder
Am I ovulating now? I see
jellyfish sacks open, release
the egg intent on its path
to the fine velour of the uterus.

I am weighed down
with my pack, my fear
of carrying a foetus through
foreign countries; the possibility
of misinterpreting morning
sickness for dysentery.

I've already decided; I won't
come home. I will have my belly
oiled with jasmine by long-haired
women, blessed by each holy man.
I will birth her without pain,
premature, and leave her, slick
and bathed in fluid, in the copper
bowl of a beggar.

BODIES FOR SCIENCE

I didn't think much about the process before you
started to cut into them, those figures robbed
of the very word – *body* –
drained of blood, faces in bags.
You assured me of the respect offered;
no music played, no cold hands waved in jest.
Just the methodical splitting open, just
your hands – as nameless as the un-body
– grasping for viscera until
you came out with the right pieces.

One day you went in for the spine.
A hundred and twenty-six students
sawed and cracked and tugged
until backbones emerged, stuck
with things you could not identify.
When the shavings settled and smell
of formaldehyde subsided, you held
sinewed links of bone, came home
later without a metaphor while I remained
intent on possible comparisons.

Cadaver, from the Latin *to fall.*
Falling into death like we fall asleep,
fall in love. What is left now
after we have fallen, pulled each other
apart, groped for the spine?
Up to our elbows we search for a centre,
for some way to explain ourselves
and the way we fell. A bleached length of bone
to point at and say, *Yes, this is it.*
Now we understand.

Each morning, we emerge bloodied,
empty-handed. Metaphors have been stretched
thin, torn by the ragged edges of longing.
Now all I ask is this: when you are about to leave,
please turn off the music,
stop waving my hand goodbye.

SEEDLING

She picks twelve, the last fruit
she will feel in her hands before leaving.
Apples, green and hard, pushed into
the chest with her clothing. *If these last
so will I.* On the boat in the dark,
they do not ripen.

After a week on the train, strangers
from her home, now called
The Old Country, greet her.
There is a farm, a fresh thatched roof,
two rooms – one theirs,
the other the kitchen, her bed
in the corner. She stores the apples
under it, prays over them, *If these ripen,
I will cede to this.* There is smoke,
cold air from open door.

They take her to church, fruit in a sack
beside her. After service, she stands on the steps
as wheat weaves yellow in every direction
and the sky bears down. She meets them
with fruit, a smell they all bend toward.
The congregation hasn't seen apples
since they came to this place.

There is one for the priest, one for the father
of each family. She falters, gives two
to the young man she could sense
behind her in the pews, her heart
branching tributaries, a small brook,
a slap in the face later at the farm.

The man will eat one apple, cut the other
to the core, pull out each seed. He will throw
all but two to the ground, remember spring.

Later, the two of them stand, shocked
and still while the camera washes them
in light – her white dress, his hands
at his sides. Their first night together,
he shows her the seedlings. *If he is kind
I will stay.* Outside, the night
is falling heavy on fields of snow.
Inside, the mattress is growing warm.

STUDY

Artists arrived at a perception of depth
as awkwardly as we all must. *Look back,*
you'll see – the figures in the distance
of sixth-century paintings are no smaller than those
pressed up against the foreground.

He explains this around a fire as light
uses our expressions to carve shadows
into faces, blankets the background flat
so that we have no context. It is here
that I first sleep with him, use no protection.
My past is a series of brush strokes, the future
something we will aim a camera at, send flares
out to capture, make real.

He is supposed to be small, far away,
retreating – yet I know we will build
fires, mark lakes and mountains
with flashbulbs until I leave again,
the memory of his body on mine
like the moment when he says *Smile!*
and I am temporarily blinded.

PART IV:
TAKEN

ು

MORE, PLEASE

The bus driver calls me friend
when I pay the fare and leave you
in street-pooled light.
He and I talk about stars
as the bus rounds corners,
careens toward a comet,
passing by us for the first time
in a thousand years.

Your first word was *moon*
and so was mine. We discovered
this over gin, drunk
with what it suggested.
Days later, we passed our first word
between us, rolling
the lunacy of our combined taste
from tongue to tongue.

Now, I ride a midnight bus away
from you. The comet trails
one thousand kisses, pricks the sky,
and light travels through me.

NOTES ON ARRIVAL /
NOTES ON LEAVING

1.   it is a transition

       over a boundary marked
       only by a fold in the map.
       now you have entered, arrived
       at a north so true the sides of the highway
       are stamped with the certainty of trees – the same
       height and width for days – announcing
       that now you are here. now you
       are here, now you are

2.   moving

       into a place where fields
       of forest give way to stone and the road
       takes on an edge, sends rocks spitting
       into crevasses, then straightens out
       just as you pass over another line,
       a border that takes you farther in,
       to where the sky opens up and bares down,
       becomes something that can press against you like

3.   his hands digging into hip;

4. a place where rivers pour

    off mountains, water crawls
    out of glaciers, spills into northern
    seas with lost ships, sunken men, the cold
    rot of skin on its spray, until it roars,
    rasp of his breath on your ear
    the only thing with which you can compare
    this sound, the insistence of it as dogged
    as day is here, day after day of light, until

5. stars puncture

    the first darkness in months.
    by then it will be time to return,

6. leave behind

    bands of humming light in sky so newly dark
    it is electric with night. when you do,
    when you leave without him, you will feel
    the fold in the map as surely as the jolt
    of tires too fast against a sudden rise
    on the road. and while

7. his smell

      wanes from your skin, you find solace
      in the fact that you have the truck, your movement
      refracted in sun off metal, a silvered drop
      sliding down the charted page, memory of his tongue
      tracing a route down your torso, thrumming south,
      the highway swelling with each town, until
      you round the last curve, a crescendo, cross
      the river's mouth to a place where the city meets itself
      on each wave and ripple the water brings in, and

8. forget everything else.

TALKING ASTRONOMY

I sense constellations here, rows of taste buds
patterned on my tongue,

but can't find them in sentences,
am embarrassed by words released

from mind to mouth, loose.
My lips, an invitation to explore;

my mouth the Stella Maris.
We tell each other how many light years

are caught in the web of sky. Time
explodes in sprays of stars, marking

our retinas in points, bright and fine.
Betelgeuse is a star wider

than the Earth's orbit around the sun
but we can't understand that kind of mass;

it has taken us both long enough to see
that bright spot as part of Orion's belt,

long enough to understand that his arrow
is not aimed at the sky but at something

larger and more ordered than points
lined up on my tongue. Something larger

than the what we won't say to each other
as we circle that silence.

CONTRACT WITH WEATHER

The surfer boys of Byron Bay, compact
in their masculinity,
bodies wetsuit-smooth statements
of intent,
have dogs who follow them,
trawl anxious shorelines
for the scent of those not-quite-men,
unquestioned lives
lived as a challenge, a contract with weather.
The dogs cast look-out on boys
who are only good
if they know that timing is everything
and we watch as well, know
that every wave swells,
expires, becomes foam coiled
around rocks, casualties
in the conspiracy of the shore,
that the possibility
of the next chance
will end with nightfall.
Oh, those surfer boys, they know
the ocean will still be there,
with its heave, ebb, and bellow,
but it will be too dark to keep
riding and late evening
rain means campfires are near

impossibilities. This is when,
if they are really good, surfer boys
will put the wet
dogs into canopied truck-beds, drive
to the nearest motel and discover
they are even better
if they realize that we too
are bodies of water;
catch the fine lip
and swell of crests,
learn to read
constantly changing conditions,
know when to get up,
when to lie low
and wait.

Lemon Fanta

The snake at the bottom of the stairs
still surprises me
when I get up in the night
to go to the toilet.
By the time I wake in the morning,
she is already gone,
in a cage strapped to the back
of Mr. Heng's moped,
on her way to the temple.

Do you like my boa?
Mr. Heng asks when he returns,
beaming up at me, hands rubbing
his belly, chest, sweat
that shines there, skin lit with heat.
His slim wife is in the kitchen
cooking me dinner.

Mr. Heng's daughters serve me
noodles and fish then watch
my tear-ducts and pores
weep with heat. I call
for Fanta, hand over mouth,
eyes watering. The girls pass me
what I ask for, unsmiling.

Can you imagine sleeping with this thing
curled around your body?
Mr. Heng asks later
when I stumble down the stairs
to wash in the courtyard shower.
No. I look at his wife
and daughters, wrapped around
each other on beds in the next room,
the blind grandmother,
cross-legged on the floor, all
laughing as they face the TV.

Mr. Heng lifts and eases
the boa back into its cage
and feeds her a banana.
She swallows it, whole,
and I am surprised
that this makes no sound.
Her throat opens
and takes in what she is fed
smoothly, silently, quick.

ONE HUNDRED DEAD KANGAROOS

Too many trips like this, backs
of vans stacked with bags, rush
to secure cooking implements
when we round sudden corners.

This van yet another, this continent
almost as large as my own but flatter,
drier, more prone to breakdowns
of all kinds. The men in the front seat
are strangers, nearly.

This isn't their country either.
Theirs is smaller, a piece of broken glass
– part of something else, all sharp edges,
something that can tear
skin, call blood to the surface.

When the motion of the back is too much,
I move up front, sit tight between
the two of them while one drives
on the wrong side of the van and the other
challenges me to a game of roadkill.

Dead animals are given numerical values,
all we have to do is spot them, marking the sides
of the road like signs, and the points are ours.
We cap the count at one hundred. I win
every time, my eye sharp for different shades of death.

Later, they leave me on the coast, turn up the radio
to news of opened gunfire, car bombs, the gaunt veneer
of their country cracked again. The farther south
I go, the fewer kangaroos I see, but I count
their dead regardless, keep my own tallies.

I will remember the heat between
our three bodies cramped in the front seat
when one of them asked, "How many points
for a dead man?" and I didn't know
how to calculate an answer.

KATE & ALLIE

Homesick, we ache
with fevers, symptoms that doctors
cannot label as one specific ailment.
Everything is evacuated, expelled
in one way or the other
and we can do nothing
but joke and groan.

We lie beside each other on single beds
in several different hotels, faces veiled
from mosquitoes like reluctant brides, gauze
of light fabric sighing under ceiling fans.
The toilets here are holes in the ground
and the sound of bucketed water means sleep
might pass like a liquid between us.

Eventually, we check into a hotel
that boasts of western toilets and televisions,
flip through channels until we hear English.
We both cry when we find *Kate and Allie*. Mothers –
North American mothers, wisecracking
and wearing pants. We stay
in the hotel for three days,
watch *Kate and Allie* nine times.

We part ways, lose symptoms, gain weight.
There is hardly a word between us
in over two years. When I see your mother
smiling from her obituary I hear
your hairbrush in each of those hotel rooms,
the strands that catch and release, your hands
working hair into braid like she did
every morning until you were twelve.

Skiing, your mother once stopped on a rise
of egg-smooth white and compared it to Heaven.
When our fevers climbed, we dreamt
of snow, of clean true north. It is we
who should be sick, sweating in hotel rooms.
Our mothers should be on the phone
to one another, the weight of ice on lines
not stopping them from telling each other
that we are all right, everything will be fine.

They are both there, waiting for spring, our return.
Our mothers are both there, the ground
glowing white in squares cut
from kitchen windows.

What is taken, then

what is lost? How much am I responsible
for giving away? Yes, I followed him
down trails, beside rivers, up slopes,
strained each muscle that moved
me. I followed, feet pounding
a rhythm with his, a series
of spent breaths that would
eventually lead us back
to the place where
we had started.

I know what I wanted. Air thrust in and out
of lungs like blows, that pure physicality,
shortness of breath, chests rising, pupils
engorged to take in the peaks
around us. Fine lick of sweat,
taste of salt on mouths, we
would always lead ourselves
back to where
we started.

To where he would leave one morning
in a sports car that denied his life
story with its two seats, not able
to carry the plot of his wife, their
children, mortgage, employment
so secure it had taken years.
My station wagon lied too,
hoodwinked at things
that weren't there.

I gear down to slow my departure
from this place. When I think
I have found the base of these
mountains, I'll stop and weep,
smarting with my own drama.
What is taken then, what is
given away, how much
am I responsible for
losing when I knew

every run through the woods would bring us
back. In my mind, he is perpetually
returning – an open door, a wife
balancing children on hip, in hand.
In my mind, I am always looking
for places where I can sleep
in the back of the car
alone, doors locked
so I will be safe.

MONTREAL 1977

Our Prime Minister, is the mother's answer
to her daughter's question, *What is charismatic?*
the word overheard as it passed between
women stationed on benches in the park.

The mothers keep words aloft, hold hands
to brows as though saluting the sky, shelter
their eyes from the sun as they safeguard
children in swinging and sliding worlds.

They share with each other what they know
of the new rules of language that their children
will soon learn in school, as though the policies are a secret,
conjugated in backrooms, entrusted to the mouths of babes.

Their children are at an age when they push
away, resist affectionate holds, and their husbands
come home with hands cramped from heaving
piles of paperwork, signing contracts all day.

In the evening, they watch him on the television,
punctuating his speech with gestures. They think of
photos of him spinning Margaret, their dance.
His hands on the paddle of a canoe.

The mothers all agree that they are glad to be there,
in that park, that city, ready for what will happen next.
When, one by one, the families move off the street, some will
move up on salaries that buck and ride the recession,

and some will move out of the province. But on that day
as they walk home from the park, the mother explains, *Charisma.
Confidence*, her daughter's hand hot in hers, *That's what we need,
what everyone wants*, and the girl takes note.

∾ Acknowledgements

Earlier versions of some of these poems appeared in *Arc, A Room of One's Own, BC Studies, Canadian Literature, Descant, Event, Ontario Review, The Amethyst Review, The Malahat Review, Vintage* 2000 and *Westerly,* and were anthologized in *The Greenboathouse Reader* (Greenboathouse Books, 1999) and *Who Lies Beautifully: The Kalamalka Anthology* (Kalamalka Press, 2002.) My sincere thanks to the editors and publishers.

Some poems were included in a chapbook of my work, *Getaway Girl,* published by Greenboathouse Books in 2002. Thank you to Jason Dewinetz, the editor and publisher, and the person who led through writing example back in the old town, back in the day.

For invaluable insight and input along the way, I would like to thank John Lent, Tom Wayman, George McWhirter, Keith Maillard, Pam Galloway, Fiona Lam and Aurian Haller. A special thanks to Marita Dachsel, Jennica Harper and Jeff Morris whose incisive and lively perceptions still resonate in many of these poems and to Nancy Lee for the cover photos and for being a constant source of inspiration, support, and glee. Thank you to my editor, Silas White, for his sharp eye and astute ear.

And, as always, I thank my family who are an amazing network of support.